Weather

Susan Koehler

Rourke
Publishing LLC
Vero Beach, Florida 32964

www.rourkepublishing.com

PHOTO CREDITS: Title Page: ©

Editor: Robert Stengard-Olliges

Cover design by Nicky Stratford, bdpublishing.com

Interior design by Renee Brady

Library of Congress Cataloging-in-Publication Data

Koehler, Susan, 1963-
  Weather / Susan Koehler.
      p. cm. -- (Let's explore science)
  Includes index.
  ISBN 978-1-60044-625-2
  1. Weather--Juvenile literature. I. Title.
  QC981.3.K62 2008
  551.6--dc22
                                        2007019957

Printed in the USA

CG/CG

Rourke Publishing

www.rourkepublishing.com – rourke@rourkepublishing.com
Post Office Box 3328. Vero Beach. FL 32964

CONTENTS

CHAPTER ONE
CHANGES IN WEATHER

Umbrellas are useful in the rain.

Should you grab an umbrella on your way out the door today? Do you need to wear a jacket? Weather conditions are always changing, and we make changes to adapt to the weather.

Weather refers to the state of the air outside. Sometimes it's cold and wet; sometimes it's warm and dry. A bright, sunny morning may be followed by a windy, cloudy afternoon.

Changes in weather are a result of the changing interactions of water, air, and **temperature** in our environment.

Watch the weather conditions in your area over the course of a week. Record the changes as they occur. Notice how often the weather is changing and be aware of the actions you take to adapt to the changing weather.

A beautiful afternoon.

Thermometers: How They Work

How does a thermometer work? A thermometer is used to measure temperature. The word thermometer is a combination of "thermo," which means heat, and "meter," which means to measure. The thermometers we commonly use are called bulb thermometers. They are usually filled with mercury, a mineral that is liquid at room temperature.

Like most liquids, mercury expands, or gets bigger, when heated. As the environment gets warmer, the expanding mercury inside the narrow glass tube of the thermometer has nowhere to go but up. When the temperature cools, the mercury slides back down the tube.

A thermometer.

Temperature is a measurement of how hot or cold we will feel in our environment. When the temperature rises, we find ways to cool off. When the temperature drops, we add layers of clothing and find heated shelters.

Although the temperature can differ greatly from one area to another and from one season to another, our temperature on Earth remains stable enough for plants and animals to live.

Sunlight

We all enjoy mild temperatures on a sunny day. However, we probably don't stop to think about just how important that sunlight is to the temperatures maintained on our planet.

The sun is the principle source of energy for our Earth. Light and heat supplied

The sun is Earths energy source.

by the sun are necessary to maintain temperatures that make our Earth inhabitable for people, plants, and animals.

A cougar.

The sun heats the air, land, and water. Heat from the sun is absorbed by the land, and the land releases heat into the air above it, even at night. Large bodies of water also store and release heat, but at a much slower rate than the land.

Areas at high altitudes, like mountaintops, are always cooler than areas at lower altitudes. Air temperatures drop more than three degrees Fahrenheit (1.6° C) with each 1,000 feet (305 m) of altitude. That's why some mountains are covered with snow year-round!

Snow is always on top of these mountains.

Whether you decide to take an umbrella with you or put on a jacket, you are finding ways to adapt to weather conditions that are continually changing.

People who live in cold climates must adapt to shoveling snow.

CHAPTER TWO

WATER IN THE EARTH SYSTEM

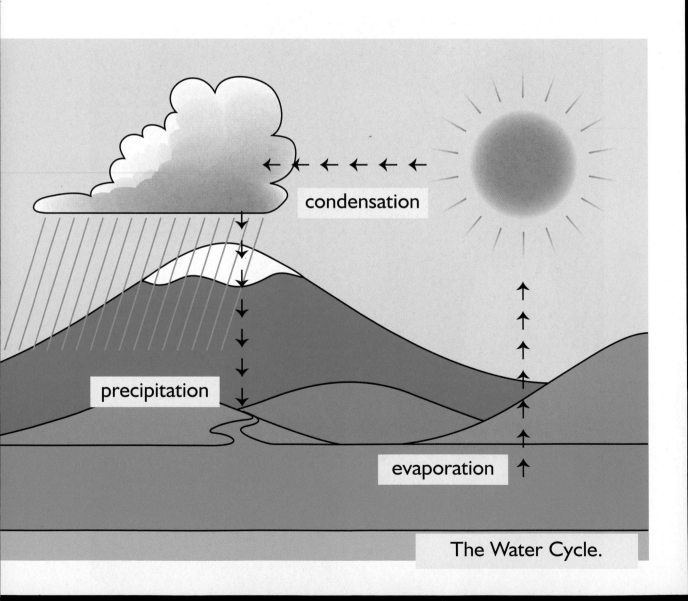

condensation

precipitation

evaporation

The Water Cycle.

The Water Cycle

You may not be able to see water all around you, but it's there. Water exists in the air in different forms and changes from one form to another. This continual process is known as the water cycle.

Water changes from a liquid to a gas form, called **water vapor**, through a process called **evaporation**. As liquid is heated by the sun's warmth, it changes into a gas form and rises in the atmosphere. In the air, water vapor cools and returns to a liquid form. This process is called **condensation**.

These water droplets cling together and form clouds. When the droplets become heavy enough, they fall to the ground as **precipitation**.

This storm cloud carries a lot of precipitation.

Rain, snow, sleet, hail

Precipitation can take on different forms, but scientists think it begins with frozen crystals in the clouds. As the crystals begin to fall and pass through warm air, they melt and become raindrops.

A rainy street.

Crystals that fall through very cold air reach the ground as snow. Sometimes the crystals begin to melt, and then refreeze. This is called sleet. Water freezes when temperatures reach 32° Fahrenheit, or 0° Celsius.

Sometimes, when strong gusts of air are present in the clouds, crystals are bounced up and down. They become coated with layer upon layer of ice until they are so heavy that they escape the gusts of air and fall to the ground as hail.

This usually happens in warmer weather, during thunderstorms. Hailstones range from less than a centimeter to several inches in size. Imagine hail the size of softballs falling from the sky!

Hailstones.

Various forms of water appear in other ways as well. When you wake up in the morning and discover drops of water covering plants, grass, and outdoor objects, this water is not the result of precipitation. These water droplets are called dew, and they are a form of condensation.

Dew drops on a vine.

At night, when temperatures drop, objects begin to cool. In the morning, as the temperature of the air is rising, many surfaces remain cool. These cool surfaces, like plants and grass, cause the water vapor in the air that surrounds them to condense and turn into liquid droplets.

Dew has gathered on these leaves.

In the same way, water condenses on the surface of windows in the morning. This is because their surfaces remain cool as the early morning temperature rises. If the temperature is below the freezing point, the droplets of liquid freeze on the cold surface and become frost.

Create Condensation

For this activity, you will need a jar with a lid and some ice cubes. Fill the jar with ice cubes and put the lid on tight. Observe the jar. After a few minutes, do you notice water droplets forming on the outside of the jar? If so, you have created condensation. The cold jar is cooling the air around it. When the air around the jar cools, water vapor in the air condenses and changes to a liquid state.

Condensation on a glass.

Early morning fog on a lake.

Fog

Have you ever walked outside on a foggy day and wondered if you were stepping into a cloud? Fog is similar to clouds because it is made of water vapor that has cooled, or condensed, to form tiny water droplets.

However, unlike clouds, fog forms from the ground up. Fog is formed when the air, which contains water vapor, is cooled by the ground or a body of water.

Sometimes you might see fog as a mist hanging over a lake. This happens because the sun is warming the air, while the lake is still cool. When the water vapor in the air is cooled by the lake's temperature, it condenses, and tiny water droplets cling together, creating fog.

Foggy mountain valleys.

Clouds

Clouds are formed in the air, because when water vapor rises from the Earth, it cools and condenses into tiny water droplets. Clouds can affect our weather. They can cool the temperature by shading us from the sun's light and heat. Precipitation occurs when clouds become saturated and the water droplets are heavy.

Common Types of Clouds

Some common types of clouds are **stratus**, **cirrus**, and **cumulus**.

Stratus clouds are low-hanging clouds that spread across the sky and cover it like a blanket. These clouds often signal gray days and possibly light rain.

Cumulus clouds are the puffy, white, cotton-candy clouds that you usually see on warm, sunny days.

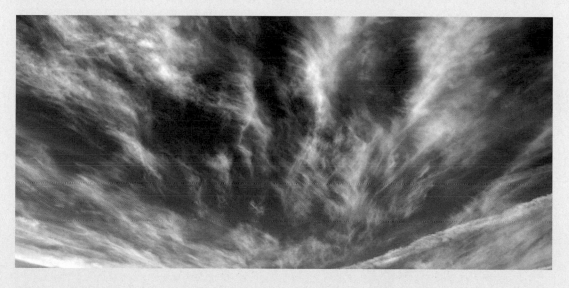

Cirrus clouds are thin and wispy. They appear high in the sky and often occur during cold weather, but usually signal that warmer weather is on the way.

CHAPTER THREE

AIR ALL AROUND US

Stretch your arms out in front of you without touching anything. Can you do it? You may not have touched an object, but your hands moved through the air, pushing it aside as they traveled. Air is the substance around us. It has weight, takes up space, and even moves around us as wind.

The air is all around you.

The Atmosphere

Like light and heat from the sun, our air is a crucial ingredient to maintaining life on our planet. The combination of gases present in our air, like oxygen, carbon dioxide, and water vapor, surround the Earth in a large belt called the **atmosphere**.

Earth's atmosphere is made of many layers. Most of the weather changes we experience are happening at the lower level of our atmosphere, called the **troposphere**.

In the troposphere, we look up and see the clouds. We feel the rain when it falls to the Earth and we sense air moving around us as wind.

Earth's atmosphere.

Our atmosphere allows sunlight to pass through and reach the ground, bringing us the light and heat we need in order to survive. Once that heat is in our atmosphere, it is trapped. That trapped heat allows the Earth to maintain temperatures suited for living things. Without our atmosphere, life on Earth would not be possible.

Without the atmosphere there would be no flowers.

Have you enjoyed the pleasure of a cool breeze on a hot day, or held tight to the string of a kite as it dipped and danced in the air above you? What causes the air to move in our atmosphere?

The wind will carry this kite.

A hurricane viewed from a satellite.

Once again, the sun plays a role in creating weather conditions. We know that wind is moving air. When the sun heats the air, it actually stirs up the movement of the air.

Wind occurs when cool air advances on warm air, or when warm air pushes against cool air. Cool air is heavier than warm air, so when the two meet, the cool air pushes itself beneath the thinner, warmer air. The warm air moves up out of the way, and the cool air slides down to replace it. This movement produces wind.

There are other factors in creating wind as well, like the Earth's rotation and orbit, the interactions of temperature and water, and the different surface features of the Earth.

Cool air pushes the warmer air up and out of th way, creating wind.

CHAPTER FOUR

SEASONS, CLIMATE, AND TEMPERATURE

The arctic has a cold climate.

Each area of the Earth has a unique climate based on the weather conditions, like temperature and precipitation, that occur over a period of time. Scientists determine the climate of an area by recording weather conditions over the course of years to create an average.

Deserts are generally dry and warm, while the tropical rain forest is warm and wet every day. Polar regions, on the other hand, are perpetually cold. These consistent patterns of temperature and precipitation determine the climate of each region.

Seasonal Change

Have you ever wondered why the weather changes with the arrival of spring, summer, winter, or fall? Seasonal changes are a direct result of the sun and our Earth's relationship with it.

Leaves changing color is a sign that fall is here.

The Earth completes its orbit around the sun in a year. As it travels through space, the Earth is tilted on its axis. If the part of the Earth where we live is tilted toward the sun, the sun's light shines directly on us and we experience the warm temperatures of summer.

When the Earth reaches the opposite side of the sun, our part of the Earth is tilted away from the sun. We still receive warmth and light, but it does not reach us directly. This causes the cooler temperatures and shorter daylight hours of winter.

Warm Rays

For this activity, you will need a globe and a flashlight. Place the globe on a flat surface. Turn on the flashlight and turn out the lights in the room. Stand about 12-18 inches (30-46 cm) from the globe and shine the flashlight directly at the equator. What difference do you notice about the amount of light shining on the equator as opposed to the poles?

Even when our part of the world is tilted toward the sun, we don't all receive equal amounts of warmth and light. The hottest parts of our Earth are located near the equator. The equator is the widest part of the Earth, so it is closer to the sun than other areas.

As the surface of the Earth curves toward the poles and away from the sun, the temperatures become cooler. That's why the North Pole and South Pole are the coldest regions of the Earth.

These differing temperatures are also responsible for a lot of our wind. Hot air near the equator rises and moves toward the poles. Heavy, cold air at the poles sinks and moves toward the equator. This cycle keeps our atmosphere in constant motion.

Heavy winds and rain take their toll on the baranches of these palm trees.

CHAPTER FOUR

STORMS

Mild precipitation and seasonal changes in weather can be easy for us to handle. However, severe weather can be a dangerous force, leaving destruction in its path.

Heavy lightning can cause power to go out.

Lightning and Thunder

Boom! Have you ever heard the rumble of thunder and wondered why it happened? Lightning, created by the electricity in clouds, heats the air around it. The air moves so suddenly that it makes a crashing sound, like an explosion. Light travels much faster than sound. That is why we often hear the thunder after we have seen the lightning. The farther away the lightning is, the longer it will take to hear the thunder.

Thunder follows lightning.

Calculate the distance of lightning

You can easily figure out about how far away lightning is from where you are. Light travels much faster than sound. You may see lightning right away, but the sound of the thunder travels five miles per second. So, when you see lightning, begin counting the seconds until you hear the thunder. "One-one thousand, two-one thousand, three-one thousand...Boom!" Stop counting when you hear the thunder. Then, divide your total seconds by five to determine about how many miles away the lightning is.

Fronts

Storms often occur when large bodies of air, called air masses, collide. Warm and cold **air masses** confront each other over the land. The place where they meet is called a **front**.

A **cold front** occurs when a cold air mass is pushing against a warm air mass. The opposite condition would be a **warm front**. A cold front moves quickly and plunges beneath warm air, often causing heavy rain or snow. These storms are usually followed by cooling temperatures. A warm front can also cause rain and temperature changes, but much more slowly.

A satellite view of a frontal system moving over the United States.

Floods

Heavy rains often bring the danger and destruction of flooding. Flash floods can occur in areas where creeks and other smaller waterways flow into larger rivers. After just a few hours of heavy rain, water levels can rise dramatically and thrust a powerful wall of water into surrounding towns.

Other floods, like **tsunamis**, can be predicted in advance. Tsunamis are giant waves caused by undersea events like Earthquakes, volcanoes, or landslides. Tsunamis, sometimes called tidal waves, can cause enormous damage to coastal areas.

Severe flooding has submerged these cars.

Tornadoes

Tornadoes are violent windstorms that occur when warm, moist air rises quickly toward cool air. Most tornadoes are funnel-shaped, but tornadoes can come in many different shapes and sizes. The rapidly swirling air occurs during a thunderstorm and stretches from the thunderstorm to the ground.

According to the National Oceanic and Atmospheric Association (NOAA), there are about 1,000 tornadoes reported in the United States each year. These tornadoes can leave a path of destruction over 1 mile (1.6 km) wide and 50 miles (80 km) long.

A tornado leaves a path of destruction.

Hurricanes

Hurricanes are severe tropical storms that form over the ocean and often travel toward land, bringing strong winds and flooding. In some parts of the world, hurricanes are called typhoons or cyclones.

Hurricanes begin as tropical storms. Wind and rain rotates in a counterclockwise direction around the "eye" of the storm. When winds reach 74 miles (119 km) per hour, the tropical storm becomes a hurricane.

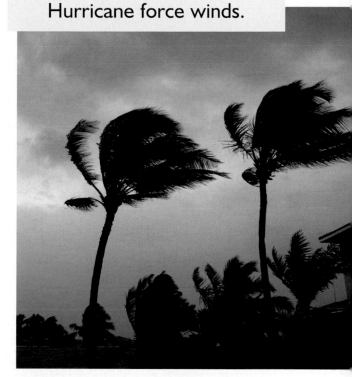
Hurricane force winds.

The aftermath of a hurricane.

Hurricanes are classified by the strength of their winds.

Categories of Hurricanes

There are five categories of hurricanes, mainly determined by the strength of the winds and the amount of potential damage to structures. It is known as the Saffir-Simpson Scale.

Category 1: 74-95 mph (119-153 km/h) winds: very limited damage to structures

Category 2: 96-110 mph (154-177 km/h) winds: generally minor damage to structures

Category 3: 111-130 mph (178-209 km/h) winds: considerable damage to small structures

Category 4: 131-155 mph (210-250 km/h) winds: considerable damage to most structures

Category 5: winds over 156 mph (251 km/h): considerable damage to structures; devastating loss to small structures and mobile homes

Blizzards

Hurricanes are confined to tropical regions, but colder areas sometimes experience dangerous winter storms called blizzards. Strong winds and snowfall create a dangerous environment where people cannot see through the blowing snow, and "whiteout" conditions often occur.

Sometimes blizzards are not made of falling snow, but of snow that has been picked up from the ground by strong winds. These storms are called ground blizzards.

Heavy blizzards can cause whiteouts.

This street and all the cars parked on it are covered in deep snow due to a blizzard.

CHAPTER FIVE

WEATHER FORECASTING

Severe storms can be very dangerous for people and animals. Long ago, storms appeared with little warning. Thanks to the science of **meteorology**, today we are able to take necessary precautions to secure our property and possibly even evacuate our homes in the days leading up to a severe storm's arrival.

Meteorology is the branch of science that studies weather and climate in our atmosphere. Meteorologists use many tools to study weather and make predictions.

A meteorologist studies a map.

Most of the instruments used by meteorologists are measurement devices. They measure the amount of precipitation that falls and the amount of moisture in the air, called **humidity**.

Thermometers

We are familiar with thermometers, which measure temperature. Thermometers are very common tools used by meteorologists.

Another instrument for measuring weather conditions is an **anemometer**. Anemometers are used to measure the speed of wind.

A **barometer** is an instrument used to measure air pressure, or the weight of air masses. Low pressure can be a sign that bad weather is on its way.

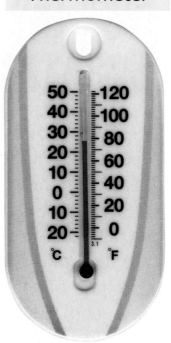

Thermometer

Anemometer

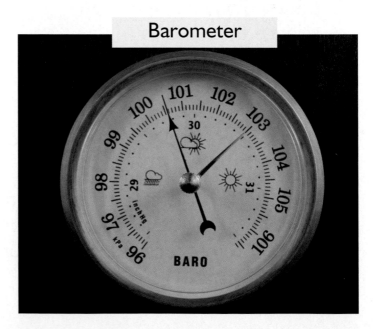

Barometer

Make your own barometer

A barometer is used to measure air pressure. You can make your own barometer with a wide-mouth jar, a balloon, a rubber band, a drinking straw and a piece of paper.

Cut the neck off of the balloon, stretch the remainder of the balloon tightly over the top of the jar, and secure it with a rubber band. Tape the straw onto the balloon surface so that about one third of it sticks out beyond the jar. Tape the paper to the wall and place the barometer so that the end of the straw points toward the paper without actually touching it. Mark the straw's height on the paper. Keep checking the straw, and each time you check, mark its height on the paper.

Over time you should see changes in the air pressure. High pressure will push the balloon's surface down, causing the straw to rise. This usually signals clear skies. Low pressure will make the balloon's surface rise, causing the straw to drop, which probably means rain.

Weather Maps

Meteorologists also use maps to track weather conditions. With maps, they are able to show people the location of storms, the temperature of various regions and the position of fronts. Weather maps are useful tools for communicating weather changes that are on the way.

Meteorological maps.

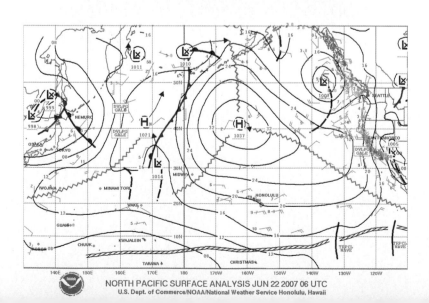

Satellites, radar, and computers are all modern devices used by meteorologists.

Satellites are launched into space and orbit the Earth. They take pictures that show weather conditions from the higher levels of Earth's atmosphere.

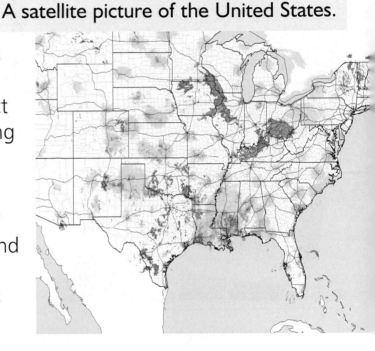

A satellite picture of the United States.

Radar uses radio waves to locate objects. Meteorologists can predict how fast a storm is moving and when it will make landfall by bouncing a signal off of rain or snow.

Computers can store and process information about weather conditions to help meteorologists make predictions.

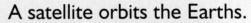

A satellite orbits the Earths.

Meteorologists often appear on television to communicate current weather conditions and to make predictions about future weather conditions. These predictions help people prepare for changes in weather.

Changing weather affects everyone. Our decisions might be simple, like whether to carry an umbrella or wear a jacket. They may be more serious decisions, like whether or not it is necessary to make preparations for dangerous and destructive weather conditions.

Weather changes constantly, but one thing always remains the same—weather affects everyone on Earth.

Questions to Consider

1. What are the three main processes of the water cycle?

2. Can you explain why we have seasons?

3. How does the science of meteorology help people?

Websites to Visit

http://www.noaa.gov
http://www.weather.gov/om/reachout/kidspage.shtml
http://eo.ucar.edu/webweather/index.html

Further Reading

Allaby, Michael. *Weather*. DK Books, 2006.
Carson, Mary Kay. *Weather Projects for Young Scientists*. Chicago Review Press, 2007.
Staub, Frank. *The Kids' Book of Clouds and Sky*. Millbrook Press, 2005.

GLOSSARY

air masses (AYR MAS es) — large bodies of air

anemometer (AN-ih-MOHM-ih-ter) — an instrument used to measure wind speed

atmosphere (AT-muhs-FEER) — the large belt of gases that surrounds the Earth

barometer (buh-ROHM-ih-ter) — an instrument used to measure air pressure

cirrus (SIR-us) — thin,wispy clouds that signal warmer weather is coming

cold front (KOLD FRUHNT) — weather that occurs when a cold air mass is pushing against a warm air mass

condensation (CON-dehn-SAY-shuhn) — the process that occurs when water vapor is cooled and changes to liquid form

cumulus (KEW-mew-lus) — puffy, white clouds usually seen on warm, sunny days

evaporation (eh-VAP-uh-RA-shuhn) — the process that occurs when heat changes liquid into vapor

front (FRUHNT) — the place where warm and cold air masses meet

humidity (hyoo-MID-ih-TEE) — moisture in the air

meteorology (ME-tee-ur-OL-oh-JEE) — branch of science that studies weather and climate in our atmosphere

precipitation (preh-SIP-ih-TAY-shuhn) — droplets of water that fall to the ground

stratus (STRAT us) — low clouds that usually signal possible rain

temperature (TEM-pur-uh-chur) — a measurement of how hot or cold our environment is

troposphere (TROP-uhs-FEER) — the lower layer of Earth's atmosphere

tsunamis (SUE-nahm-eez) — giant waves that hit land as a result of an undersea earthquake, volcanic eruption, or landslide

warm front (WAHRM FRUHNT) — weather that occurs when a warm air mass is pushing against a cold air mass

water vapor (WAH tur VAY pur) — the gas form of water

INDEX

About the Author

Susan Koehler is a teacher and a writer who lives in Tallahassee, Florida with her husband, five children, three cats and one dog.